KT-162-052

PROSECCO MADE ME DO IT

PROSECCO MADE ME DO IT

60 SERIOUSLY SPARKLING COCKTAILS

AMY ZAVATTO
ILLUSTRATED BY RUBY TAYLOR

HarperCollins*Publishers*

HarperCollins*Publishers*
1 London Bridge Street
London SE1 9GF
www.harpercollins.co.uk

First published by HarperCollins*Publishers* in 2017

10 9

Copyright © HarperCollins*Publishers*
Written by Amy Zavatto
Illustrated by Ruby Taylor
Designed by Eleanor Ridsdale

A catalogue record for this book is available from the British Library

ISBN 978-0-00-826017-0

Printed and bound in Latvia

MIX
Paper from
responsible sources
FSC
www.fsc.org   **FSC™ C007454**

CONTENTS

INTRODUCTION

The year is 1868. Louisa May Alcott's classic *Little Women* is first published. Australia ends its era as a penal colony for England. African American men gain the right to vote in the United States. The first cro-magnon human remains are unearthed by French geologist Louis Lartet. And Antonio Carpané produces the very first bottle of sparkling Prosecco, gleaned from the breezy hills of Conegliano and Valdobbiadene in northern Italy.

Carpané could only have dreamt that, by the beginning of the 21st century, his fizzy, frothy experiment would become the most toasted of toastables the world over. And why not? Affordable Prosecco makes bubbles accessible. For years, sparkling wine was relegated to the special occasion – the wedding toast, the birth, the big job promotion, the holidays, but… what about all those other days during the year when a glass of something sparkly performs the happy miracle of putting a smile on your face? Prosecco whets the appetite, enlivens the senses with its beautiful, fruity aromatics and makes a spectacular date at the dinner table.

From the traditional Bellini (see page 27) to the sophisticated Ship to Shore (see page 56), Prosecco adds lift and life. When paired with anything from juices to fortified aperitifs, it can be an easy two-ingredient tipple that you can whip up in seconds. When combined in a multi-ingredient cocktail, it elevates flavours and aromatics with its freshness and zippy bubbles. Like mustard, butter and milk, it really should be in your refrigerator at all times.

Prosecco Made Me Do It is going to get you into that frame of mind ('Oh, a snowstorm's coming ? Better get Prosecco!'). These 60 cocktails – from the easy-peasy and riffs on classics to entirely new-to-this-world creations – will not only become entertaining staples for your home bar, but if I have my way, they'll inspire you to come up with your own variations with this most charming of Italian sparkling wines, too. Let the Champagne drinkers hoard their bottles for a moment that never comes. Prosecco drinkers have more fun.

COSA È PROSECCO?

'What is Prosecco?'

I used to get this question a lot. Along with:
'It's Champagne, right?'
'It's sweet, right?'
'It's just cheap stuff, right?'

Then, it seems, the world at large had an 'Ah-ha!' moment, and Prosecco was everywhere. A glass of Prosecco before dinner? Well, of course! A low-alcohol spritz to whet your whistle when out for drinks with friends? Absolutely! Wine lists and cocktail menus began to burst with options for the Italian fizzy stuff. And yet… the 'What is Prosecco?' question lingers. It's popular! It's fun! It's Italian! What else do you need to know? It's all the same, right? Like anything, if it's worth the pleasure it provides when it passes your lips, it's worth learning a little bit about because, inevitably, those little bubbles of knowledge will help you make great choices – and, therefore, drink really well. Is Prosecco inexpensive? In comparison to high-end Champagne (which, by the way, can only be called that if it's made in the Champagne region using traditional methods), yes. But whether you're spending a little or a lot, you should know what you're getting. And that's what we're going to dive into here. What is Prosecco? Glad you asked…

PLACE OF POP

Prosecco is the name of the DOC (*denominazione di origine controllata*) – a regional designation which, when you see it on a wine label, is a way of assuring you that the product you are buying is made from certain ingredients in a particular place and in a certain way. It's a thumbs-up for hitting basic standards of quality. Groovy, right?

In the case of Prosecco, that place in question is about as north-east as you can go, reaching across the regions of Veneto to Friuli Venezia Giulia near the Adriatic Sea, and rimmed to the north by the Dolomite Mountains and the eastern rim of the Alps. Most wines from this broad area are designated as DOC on the label, but there are also three other special designations within it that speak to an even higher guaranteed level of quality and site specificity.

The first two are Treviso and Trieste. If you see either of those places listed on the label of your DOC-level Prosecco, that means the grapes and production happened within those specific areas.

There is a third zone, however, that the Italian government gave an even more special designation: the Conegliano Valdobbiadene DOCG (*denominazione di origine controllata e garantita*). That G? That means, along with all the other assurances like specific region and grape, the government is *guaranteeing* the actual quality of what you're about to drink. That's pretty cool!

Another one of those DOC standards is the grape or grapes that can be used: Glera grapes, which, for a while, were also called Prosecco. (So if you thought Prosecco was the actual name of the grape, don't feel bad.) All wines labelled as Prosecco must be made up of 85% of this Italian white grape variety, which is more often than not rife with beautiful orchard fruit notes. What's the other 15%? About five or so other indigenous white varieties (if you really want to know: Glera Tonda, Glera Lunga, Glera Verdiso, Glera Perera and Glera Bianchetta Trevigiana), and, since the 1960s, four international grape varieties: Chardonnay, Pinot Grigio, Pinot Bianco and Pinot Nero (or Noir, as you may know it better).

There are three ways the DOC permits Prosecco producers to make their bubbly, but by and large what you buy from your favourite local wine shop or supermarket is in the spumante style, which is super bubbly (there's also frizzante, with its more gentle bubbles, and a completely non-bubbly version, tranquilo).

THE DL ON THE DOCG
It's worth taking a closer look at Conegliano Valdobbiadene, as it is a concentrated, unique little spot. I know – it's super hard to say, so let's begin with a little phonetic pronunciation lesson: cone-ell-yanno. Not so hard, right? Next up: val-doe-be-ah-den-ay. That one's a little

trickier. But if you practice a few times, it'll start to roll around your tongue and out of your mouth like you're a real Italian. And, you know, who doesn't want to sound like a real Italian? I sure do.

Conegliano Valdobbiadene is a special place. It's home to the birthplace of Prosecco wine, where the oldest vines dwell on dizzyingly steep south-facing slopes, and only the gentle human hand can carefully pick the fruit. Here, the vines are warmed by the sun and cooled by the breezes off the Adriatic Sea, and sit in diverse plots of land that make for beautifully nuanced sparkling wines. Grapes have likely been grown here for thousands of years, but it's the late 20th century where things start getting really exciting for Prosecco.

In 1962, 11 local guys got together and said, you know, this place is pretty special! They formed the *Consorzio di Tutela del Prosecco di Conegliano e Valdobbiadene*. By 1969, the Italian government came around to agreeing (things take time in Italy – long lunches and all) and recognized the area as part of its special DOC system of quality.

But all along, Prosecco had been slowly but surely becoming more popular, thanks in part to Guiseppe Cipriani. Cipriani opened the famed Harry's Bar near the Piazza San Marco in Venice in 1931. It was here that he created a cocktail that not only outlasted his own life, but perhaps will still be poured long after the sea claims Venice for its own: the Bellini (see page 27). The irresistible mix of fresh white peach purée and Prosecco was a hit with both aristocrats and American soldiers stationed in Italy. They brought the drink to the US and, by the late 1960s, Prosecco began to appear in America; it had already crossed borders into other parts of Europe. Demand increased, and thus did production.

Fast forward to the noughties, and Glera growing and Prosecco making had spread far beyond the Congeliano-Valdobbiadene (C-V) borders into two full-on regions, nine provinces and 556 villages. Prosecco, you see, is prolific. Grapes were being planted in the valleys, where they grew fast and loose and harvesting could be done with quick-grabbing machines, allowing more, more, more Prosecco to fill glasses the world over. The problem with that: it diluted the quality. How could you tell the difference between a hand-harvested complex Prosecco from the C-V hills and a fast and loose fandango, machine-harvested in the valley?

Up until the turn of the 20th century, the bubbles in Prosecco (and Champagne) were happening in the bottle via something called secondary fermentation. Fermentation is, simply, how alcohol happens: yeast (which exists naturally, or can be added) eats sugar (which, voila! is in grapes) and you get alcohol. You get bubbles when a second fermentation happens within a small space, like a bottle. This was happening with Prosecco, but not with totally reliable results. Some bottles were more sparkly than others. Some were still wines. And some bottles even exploded. Yikes.

In 1895, a brilliant man named Federico Martinotti figured out how to make a more reliable bubbly product with the region's beloved Glera grapes. If that second fermentation could happen in large, pressurized wooden tanks, it could be better controlled. But it still wasn't totally reliable. Another smart person named Eugene Charmat came along a few years later, tinkered with Martinotti's technique, and invented a new tank in a more reliable material (stainless steel), that seemed pretty foolproof. And thus, the Charmat Method, by which nearly all Prosecco is produced, was born. Ta-da!

About 90 million bottles a year come from the DOCG zone, which is about 30 kilometres at its widest with around 7,000 hectares planted. So, that's about one case of Prosecco per year for every person living in Amsterdam or Hong Kong. Lucky them! But compare that to 420 million bottles coming out of the greater DOC area and about 20,000 hectares, and you start to get the picture. This is why in 2009 the government awarded C-V the special status of DOCG. When you pick up a bottle, this will be clearly stated on the label, along with the word 'superiore', just for that extra-special emphasis. And for what it's worth, just outside of the western tip of Conegliano Valdobbiadene is a little (just shy of 200 hectares) spot called Asolo, which is another separate Prosecco DOCG adhering to the same parameters and standards of quality that C-V does. But within C-V, things actually get even more wine-geeky, so let's break it down…

Conegliano Valdobbiadene Prosecco Superiore

The oldest Prosecco producing spot, this DOCG was born (or, well, re-born) in 2009 to set its particularity apart from the rest of the Prosecco wines.

Rive

A super-special sub-zone designation, not unlike the villages of Burgundy. There are currently 43 in total. If you see this word along with Conegliano Valdobbiadene Prosecco Superiore, it means the grapes come only from the rive named on the label. The other cool thing about that: it positions you a little deeper into the region, letting you know if the grapes in your juice are from the more dense soils of Conegliano, which tend to give you a little more richness in texture, or the shallow, rocky soils of Valdobbiadene, rife with marine-deposits. Wines from here tend to have more prominent floral and minerally notes and, call me crazy, but a little bit of that seaside salinity, too.

Cartizze

Let's just call this Prosecco Oz. It's a single little 107-hectare area within Valdobbiadene in the western reaches of the DOCG.

SWEET (AND NOT-SO-SWEET) SENSATIONS

As you learned above, all Prosecco is not created equal. So it's kind of funny how it got a rep for being sweet. Some are, sure, but certainly not all. How can you know? That's easy. Regardless of where your Prosecco came from within the region (or the region within the region within the region!), every bottle has a wonderful, simple clue. If your bottle says:

Extra Brut

This designation is pretty new (made official as of 2017, although certainly wines had been made in the past at this level of dryness), and means there are between 0 and 6 grams of sugar in the final product. If you like your sparkly dry like a cracker, this one's for you.

Brut

This used to be the catch-all for extra brut, too, but now means you're at a dry 6–12 grams of sugar. Nice and dry.

Extra Dry

At 12–17 grams of sugar, this might seem a little confusing. Shouldn't 'extra dry' mean… extra dry? Maybe, but it doesn't – it means the Prosecco in question has a nice easy-going bit of sweetness to it, but isn't cloying or over-the-top. When you're working with cocktails in which you want to play up the fruity essence in the drink, this is where you want to go.

Dry

At 17–32 grams of sugar, this not-so-dry sparkling is in the dessert zone. And if you don't have any simple syrup or bar sugar on hand, it can be great to play around with if you need just that little bit of extra sweetness to balance out other more savoury or sour notes.

You'll notice in the recipes that I steer you towards one or another of these sweetness levels. That's worth paying attention to. Like any cocktail ingredient, you should consider what it brings to the final result. Some more juniper-heavy, herbaceous gins, for instance, make for an excellent Martini, while other more citrus-forward versions are key to a refreshing gin and tonic. Opt for one sweet vermouth or another, and your Manhattan takes on a whole new dimension. Same with Prosecco.

TOP TIPS

You now know how Prosecco came to be. You know where it's from and the nuances of the region and can walk into any wine shop and pick like a pro! But before we jump into all the fun that's to come, let's go over a few basics to help set your Prosecco-cocktail concocting on a good path.

HOW TO OPEN A BOTTLE

Put that sabre away, and for the love of Pete, DO NOT ever launch a cork into the atmosphere. The former is for the pros and the latter is just a silly, dangerous thing to do, no matter how fun it might seem. When you hit your best friend in the eye with a cork powered by 2.5 bars of pressure, I guarantee they will not be happy with you.

So do this instead:
1. Set the bottle on a solid surface, like a worktop.
2. Grab a tea towel or kitchen towel.
3. Place the towel over the top of the bottle.
4. Grab the base of the bottle securely with one hand, and put the other hand over the top of the towel-covered cork section.
5. Gently twist until the cork is released.

That's it. I swear, it's really easy. You won't lose tons of overflowing delicious Prosecco and no one gets hurt. No better way to get the party started right.

STORING YOUR WINE

Like any wine, store your Prosecco in a cool, dark, mildly humid place (like a basement, if you have one) on its side until you're ready to chill it and use it. Do not store it or any other wine for the long term in the refrigerator – the opening and closing of the door makes for lots of up and down in temperature and its just too dry of an atmosphere for the long haul with any wine. Definitely do not store your bottles on top of the refrigerator, or any high-up area – heat rises! Heat is the enemy of wine, and definitely the arch rival of bubbles.

When ready to use your Prosecco, pop it in the fridge a few hours or up to a day or so beforehand.

It might sound bananas, but if you don't manage to finish an opened bottle (blasphemous!), use a simple Champagne stopper – these have a rubber seal that you press into the lip of the bottle and two side wings that fasten onto the rim. They're inexpensive, easy to find and you can use them for beer and cider, too.

INGREDIENT CARE

Aside from spirits, cocktails require other ingredients, like fruits, herbs and sweeteners like syrups.

When it comes to fruit, the number one rule: always wash it! By wash, I mean rinse thoroughly with cool water. That goes for citrus, especially if you're using the zest as a garnish. With raspberries and blackberries, only gently rinse what you need – washing all of them at once and putting back the brunt that isn't going to go in your cocktail will lead to mouldy fruit. All those little bumps and nooks and crannies hold the moisture and, thus, start to rot faster when wet. Blueberries and strawberries are an exception, but you should let them dry off on a towel before putting them back in your refrigerator.

As for herbs, gently rinse and pat dry. Store any extra, like flowers, with the stems in a container of water, or dampen a paper towel, wrap them up and store in the crisper of your refrigerator.

SYRUPS

Many cocktails in this book require a touch of simple syrup.
I prefer using this to caster sugar or any granulated sugar,
no matter how fine, because it's already dissolved and easier
to mix with. Make a batch ahead of time and store it in your
refrigerator. The variations you can make on this are only
limited by your imagination and ingredients, but here are
the recipes contained in this book for your reference.

SIMPLE SYRUP

The basic recipe tells you a lot about the name:
it's simple! The method is as follows:
One part sugar to one part water.

Combine the sugar and water in a small saucepan over a
medium heat and gently stir until the sugar dissolves. Leave to
cool, then store in an airtight container for up to 2 weeks.

MINT SIMPLE SYRUP

200g (7oz) granulated white sugar
240ml (8fl oz) water
5g (⅛oz) fresh mint leaves, washed

Drop the mint into a small saucepan and gently muddle to release the
oils. Add the sugar and water and cook over a medium heat. Gently
stir until the sugar dissolves and the aroma of the mint is prominent.
Leave to cool, then store in an airtight container for up to 2 weeks.

VARIATIONS

Basil Simple Syrup – make as above but use basil instead of mint.
Rosemary Simple Syrup – make as above but use 3–4 fresh
rosemary sprigs instead of mint.

Cinnamon Simple Syrup – combine 3 cinnamon sticks in the saucepan with the sugar and water and continue as before.
Honey Syrup – combine 240ml (8fl oz) honey with the water in a saucepan and continue as before.
Honey-Basil Syrup – combine 240ml (8 fl oz) honey and 5g (⅛oz) fresh basil leaves with the water and continue as before.
Ginger Simple Syrup – cook the sugar and water as before and add a 125g (4oz) piece of ginger, peeled and very thinly sliced. Bring to a simmer, remove from the heat and leave to steep for 30 minutes. Pour through a fine-mesh sieve into an airtight container.

CONCORD GRAPE SYRUP

The sweetness inherent in grapes means no sugar need apply. Simply take 150g (5oz) rinsed Concord grapes (although any red or black grapes will do) and put them in a small saucepan. Cook over a medium heat, stirring, until the grape skins begin to break and the juice and flesh spill out into the pan. Cook down for about 5 minutes. Cool and press through a fine mesh sieve, discarding the extra pulp, skins and stems. Store in an airtight container for up to 2 weeks.

GRENADINE

Sure, you can buy it, but it won't taste half as good (and will likely have high-fructose corn syrup in the mix – yuck).

240ml (8fl oz) unsweetened pomegranate juice
200g (7oz) granulated white sugar
1 tsp rose water

Combine the pomegranate juice, water and rose water in a small saucepan over a medium heat and gently stir until the sugar dissolves. Leave to cool, then store in an airtight container for up to 2 weeks.

PURÉES

There is no Bellini without peach purée. But, as a matter of fact, purées in general are a great cocktail ingredient, and specifically make a delicious dance partner for fruit-centric Prosecco. To keep the fruit from oxidizing, add a little lemon juice into the mix to help hold the colour of the pretty fruit and keep it fresher longer.

WHITE PEACH PURÉE
450g (1lb) ripe white peaches, washed and cut into
   quarters, stones discarded
30ml (1fl oz) freshly squeezed lemon juice
45ml (1½fl oz) Simple Syrup (see page 16)

Purée all the ingredients in a blender or food processor until very smooth. Freeze or store in the refrigerator in an airtight container for up to a week.

VARIATIONS
Really anything goes in terms of fruits, so try using your favourite and experiment. Here are a few used in the book:

Strawberry Purée – make as above but use 400g (14oz) washed, hulled and halved strawberries, 22ml (¾fl oz) freshly squeezed lemon juice and 30ml (1fl oz) Simple Syrup (see page 16).

Spiced Pear Purée – make as above but use 450g (1lb) ripe Conference pears, washed and quartered, 30ml (1fl oz) freshly squeezed lemon juice and 45ml (1½fl oz) Cinnamon Simple Syrup (see page 17). To make this extra spicy, add a little star anise into the pan when you're making your Cinnamon Simple Syrup.

Watermelon Purée – make as above but use 300g (10½oz) cubed watermelon, 15ml (½fl oz) freshly squeezed lemon or lime juice and 30ml (1fl oz) Simple Syrup (see page 16).

ICE-CAPADES!

Ice is important in cocktails. Some bartenders might even tell you it's the most important ingredient. If your ice is old and smelly (yes, I'm talking to you, person who hasn't cleaned out their freezer in a really, really, really long time), your drink will reflect that nastiness. At the very least, make sure your ice is the product of a good environment.

Ice adds cold, obviously. But ice also adds the very important component of dilution. When it comes to punches, you do not want to add a pile of ice cubes – they will melt faster than you can pop your Prosecco, and ruin a perfectly good mass-scale drink. Instead, make an ice ring or ice block.

It's simple to do: fill a clean bundt pan or large plastic storage container with water. Put it in your freezer a good 24 hours prior to your party.

To release the ice, run under cold (not hot!) water for a minute and then gently shake out into your punch bowl. That's it. It will dissolve much more slowly – and look pretty cool, too.

Up the ante by taking the garnish suggestions in the punch recipes starting on page 130 and drop them into the water of your ice ring before freezing. Voila – floating garnishes suspended in animation!

THE RECIPES

VENETIAN SPRITZ

The first time I had this refreshing, super-easy aperitif was not, as the name might imply, in Venice. It was in Red Hook, Brooklyn, one of the earlier settlements in New York City's history as an American Revolution point of defence and, eventually, a bustling port. The bar where the Venetian Spritz first passed my lips is called Fort Defiance, named for the stalwart spot that defended the area during the Battle of Long Island. But there was no battle when I sipped this lovely pre-dinner quencher. Aperol is a bitter Italian liqueur, lower in alcohol and a little sweeter than its similarly red-hued cousin, Campari. For that reason, it makes a lovely complement to Prosecco's typical orchard fruitiness. A brut-style balances the Aperol nicely. The olive? I was dubious, too, the first time I had this cocktail. But there was something about the sweet and sour that appealed to my cocktail-subversive side. If you are not so keen, feel free to simply sip this as-is, or with an orange slice.

Ingredients

45ml (1 ½fl oz) Aperol
90ml (3fl oz) brut-style Prosecco
a splash of soda water
1 Cerignola olive, red or green – your choice (optional)

Instructions

Fill a double rocks glass with ice. Pour in the Aperol followed by the Prosecco. Give it a little stir. Top up with a splash of soda water and garnish with a Cerignola olive.

PROSECCO SABA

The island of Sardinia sits off the west coast of Italy, its
west and southern borders facing the Mediterranean
Sea, the Tyrrhenian Sea to the east, and the Strait of
Bonifacio separating its northern shores from Corsica.
As it goes on islands, Sardinia maintains many unique
particularities, like its language, Sardo – a mix of Latin,
Arabic, Spanish and Catalan – which tells you a lot about
what a coveted spot Sardinia was before Italy claimed it
for its own. Saba is one of the island's many unique little
treasures. This sweet-tart, silky condiment is the product
of cooked-down grape must (that is, the leftover juice,
skins, stones and stems after crushing). An extra dry-style
Prosecco plays up the saba and makes a great aperitif.

Ingredients
8ml (¼fl oz) Saba
90ml (3fl oz) extra dry-style Prosecco

Instructions
Drizzle the Saba into a tulip glass, then slowly top
with the Prosecco. Give it a little stir and serve.

BELLINI (TRADITIONAL)

One of the great things about Prosecco as a cocktail ingredient is that your choice of two-ingredient, ridiculously easy to whip up concoctions are nearly endless – as are the variations on what is perhaps the most famous of two-ingredient Prosecco cocktails: the Bellini. Famously invented by the owner of Harry's Bar in Venice, Giuseppe Cipriani, the drink originally calls for white peaches, but if all you have are beautiful, ripe yellow peaches, that's just fine, too.

Ingredients
30ml (1fl oz) White Peach Purée (see page 18)
90ml (3fl oz) brut-style Prosecco

Instructions
Pour the White Peach Purée into a flute. Top with the Prosecco, give it a little stir and serve.

TROPICAL BELLINI

It's Saturday night. The air is balmy, but a beautiful breeze drifts through your window. If you call up some fado on your iPod and close your eyes, you can almost conjure up that vacation you took last year to the beaches of Brazil. Better yet, make one of these. Passion fruit are native to South America. Use the instructions on page 18 to make your own purée, or else feel perfectly free to seek out a high-quality bottled version at your local gourmet food shop (as straining out the edible seeds through a sieve from the fresh version might put a dampener on your nice daydream).

Ingredients
30ml (1fl oz) passion fruit purée
90ml (3fl oz) brut-style Prosecco

Instructions
Pour the passion fruit purée into a flute. Top with the Prosecco, give it a little stir and serve.

DRINK ROSSINI

SPECIAL

PROSECCO

ROSSINI

While you can find strawberries in supermarkets all
year round, there's really nothing so wonderful as that
aromatic moment in early summer when tiny, fresh local
strawberries are at their fleeting, seasonal peak. Always
rinse them before setting to work removing the green
tops and cutting them up for puréeing. This drink was
named for the Italian composer Gioacchino Rossini,
whether because of his penchant for fine food and drink,
or for the bubbly character of his music, who can say.

Ingredients
30ml (1fl oz) Strawberry Purée (see page 18)
90ml (3fl oz) extra dry-style Prosecco

Instructions
Pour the Strawberry Purée into a flute. Top with the Prosecco,
give it a little stir and serve.

AUTUMN BELLINI

There's always a ton of talk about what wine to serve
for the eat-until-you-pop Thanksgiving holiday in the
United States. But I like to make sure I start my family and
friends off with something festive when they walk in the
door; something that makes them smile, slow down and
get in the holiday mood. This easy-peasy, spicy sparkling
cocktail makes a great kick-off to any epic celebration.

Ingredients
30ml (1fl oz) Spiced Pear Purée (see page 18)
90ml (3fl oz) extra dry-style Prosecco
1 slender slice of pear, to garnish

Instructions
Pour the Spiced Pear Purée into a flute. Top with the Prosecco.
Give it a little stir and garnish with the pear slice.

SOUTHERN LIFE

Sweet Marsala (and, well, the dry version, too), from the area surrounding the eponymous city in Sicily, got kind of a bad rep for a while. You know, it became the kind of thing grannies drank from tiny glasses when they were feeling a little special. Well, with age comes wisdom – Marsala is delicious – and a multitude of bartenders have discovered its layered, complex charms in cocktails the world over. This southern Italian speciality, with its aromas and flavours of walnuts and dried fruit, adds a sophisticated note to the basic ingredients of a Bellini – peach purée and Prosecco (see page 27).

Ingredients
30ml (1fl oz) White Peach Purée (see page 18)
22ml (¾fl oz) sweet Marsala wine
90ml (3fl oz) extra brut-style Prosecco

Instructions
Pour the White Peach Purée into a tulip glass. Add the Marsala and top with the Prosecco. Give it a little stir to keep the purée from settling on the bottom of the glass and serve.

FRAGOLA FIZZ

The key to this drink is giving your strawberries a good mashing – because you'll be sipping it with a straw, you don't want any getting stuck on the way up, so make sure you get all those solid pieces beneath your muddler! The fruitiness natural to Prosecco takes all those delicious strawberry aromatics and flavours to another level.

Ingredients
4 medium (or 3 large) strawberries, quartered
15ml (½fl oz) Mint Simple Syrup (see page 16)
15ml (½fl oz) freshly squeezed lemon juice
30ml (1fl oz) vodka
90–120ml (3–4fl oz) brut-style Prosecco

Instructions
Drop the strawberries into a Collins glass, pour in the Mint Simple Syrup and muddle until very pulpy. Add the lemon juice and vodka. Fill with ice, top with the Prosecco and give it a little stir to evenly distribute the mashed-up berries. Finish with a straw.

CLIMB EVERY MOUNTAIN

Pisco is a South American brandy made in both Peru and Chile that's distilled from crushed, fermented grapes (up to eight kinds in the mix!). Its calling card is the delightful Pisco Sour – a frothy frolic of a cocktail composed of Pisco, lime juice, simple syrup, egg white and a swirl of Angostura bitters. But brandy and Prosecco? Oh, they like each other a lot, perhaps because they both have grapes at their core. Mix with a little orange-y, bitter-sweet Amaro Montenegro liqueur, and it makes for a fine low-alcohol, sophisticated sipper.

Ingredients
30ml (1 fl oz) Pisco
22ml (¾fl oz) Amaro Montenegro liqueur
60ml (2fl oz) brut-style Prosecco
a wide piece of orange peel, to garnish

Instructions
Pour the Pisco and Amaro Montenegro into an ice-filled double rocks glass. Stir well. Top with the Prosecco and garnish with the orange peel.

SBAGLIATO

Mistakes have a bad rep as being the result of a good thing gone wrong. But in the case of the *Sbagliato* (or 'mistaken' in Italian), a wrong bottle made for a right cocktail. So the story goes: a bartender attempting to produce a hasty Negroni picked up a bottle of Prosecco instead of gin. And so, a lovely, lip-smacking aperitif was born. Although a Negroni calls for equal parts of its ingredients, I like to add a little more Prosecco to mine.

Ingredients

30ml (1fl oz) Campari
30ml (1fl oz) sweet vermouth
60ml (2fl oz) brut-style Prosecco
a wide piece of orange peel, to garnish

Instructions

Pour the Campari, sweet vermouth and Prosecco into an ice-filled double rocks glass. Give it a little stir and garnish with the orange peel.

SBAGLIATO 2

When the snow melts and the weather starts to turn a little nice, my husband often makes requests for cocktails that have a little fizz to them. He's a Negroni devotee, and one night when I was mixing one for myself, I offered him the same. 'It sounds nice', he said, 'but… I kinda want something with a little effervescence to it; a little pop'.

If a Sbagliato was indeed the result of a Negroni gone awry, why not put it back on the proper path and just add a little sparkle? It's become a hit around our house when a stirred drink needs just a little oomph on a Friday night.

Ingredients
22ml (¾fl oz) Campari
22ml (¾fl oz) sweet vermouth
22ml (¾fl oz) gin
30ml (1fl oz) brut-style Prosecco
a wide piece of orange peel, to garnish

Instructions
Pour the Campari, sweet vermouth, gin and Prosecco into an ice-filled double rocks glass. Give it a little stir and garnish with the orange peel.

SPARKLING CRUSTA

New Orleans, Louisiana, is the birthplace of some of the
world's best cocktails – the Sazerac, the Vieux Carre, the
Ramos Gin Fizz, the Brandy Crusta. The latter offers up a
whole lot of flavour and the sweet treat of a sugared rim,
making it a great brunch, party or post-dinner sipper.
I like to play up the fruitiness of the Cognac with fig bitters
instead of Angostura, as is traditional. Also, because
there's a lot of liqueur components to this drink, I opt for
a drier brut-style Prosecco to balance out the elements.

Ingredients

45ml (1 ½fl oz) Cognac VS
8ml (¼fl oz) Luxardo Maraschino liqueur
8ml (¼fl oz) triple sec
15ml (½fl oz) freshly squeezed lemon juice
  (reserving the squeezed out lemon)
8ml (¼fl oz) Simple Syrup (see page 16)
2–3 dashes of fig bitters
30–60ml (1–2fl oz) brut-style Prosecco
granulated sugar, to rim the glass
a lemon twist, to garnish

Instructions

Combine the Cognac, Luxardo Maraschino liqueur, triple
sec, lemon juice, Simple Syrup and fig bitters in a shaker filled
with ice and shake well. Rub the inside of the squeezed-out
lemon around the rim of a coupe or cocktail glass. Sprinkle
the sugar onto a flat plate and dip in the edges of the glass
to coat the rim. Strain the contents of the shaker into the
glass, top with Prosecco and garnish with the lemon twist.

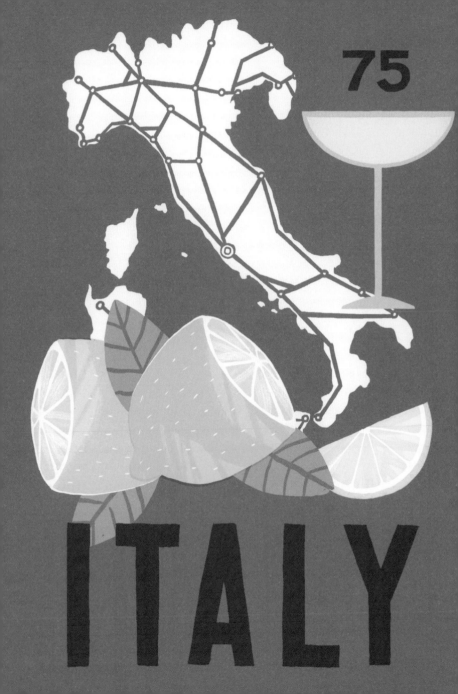

ITALIAN 75

Why should Champagne have all the fun? An elegant staple of the Sunday morning set, the French 75's origins are a bit murky (as many cocktail births are), but it seems to have had its pop-the-cork creation sometime during World War I. Another fogged up lens into the past obscures whether the drink should be made with gin or Cognac, a debate that continues to rage. What is clear is that the 75 is unequivocal proof that the notion of adding sparkling (like in our souped-up Negroni on page 43) to a standard isn't a new idea, but a good one that's been in use for quite some time. For all intents and purposes, this drink begins as a sour, just one that gets a little extra zip via, in this case, Prosecco.

Ingredients
45ml (1½fl oz) Cognac
15ml (½fl oz) freshly squeezed lemon juice
15ml (½fl oz) Simple Syrup (see page 16)
60ml (2fl oz) brut-style Prosecco
a lemon twist, to garnish

Instructions
Pour the Cognac, lemon juice and Simple Syrup into an ice-filled cocktail shaker. Shake well and strain into a coupe or cocktail glass. Top with the Prosecco and garnish with the lemon twist.

CHEERS TO SAL

New York City is full of southern Italian immigrants and their descendants who came by the millions between the 19th and 20th centuries (my own grandfather, grandmother and aunts arrived in the 1920s, citizens already as my grandfather fought on the side of the Americans in World War I). My friend Tina's dad arrived towards the end of the great move of southern Italians and Sicilians to New York. One of his favourite things to sip on before dinner was a little Amaro Averna and Prosecco: a lovely bitter-fruity combo if there ever was one. The story goes that credit for the creation of Averna's liqueur is owed to Salvatore Averna, who was given the recipe by the monks of his local abbey in Caltanissetta, Sicily.

Ingredients
45ml (1 ½fl oz) Amaro Averna liqueur
90ml (3fl oz) extra dry-style Prosecco

Instructions
Pour the Averna into a flute and top with the Prosecco. Alternatively, you can also serve this over ice in a rocks glass.

SICILIAN
Spritz

PROSECCO
MT ETNA
D.O.C.
13% abv   750ml

SICILIAN SPRITZ

I took the previous drink and tweaked it a little, using the concept of the spritz and Champagne cocktail to come up with something that I love to offer friends and guests to whet their appetites before dinner. I like using a brut-style Prosecco here, but if you prefer to tip this drink more towards the sweeter side, go for a dry style.

Ingredients
1 sugar cube
4–5 dashes of orange bitters
22ml (¾fl oz) Amaro Averna liqueur
60–90ml (2–3fl oz) brut-style Prosecco
a splash of soda water
a wide piece of orange peel, to garnish

Instructions
Drop a sugar cube into a double rocks glass and splash it with the orange bitters. Crush with a muddler or a wooden spoon. Add the Amaro Averna, fill with ice and pour in the Prosecco. Give it a little stir, top with a splash of soda water and garnish with the orange peel.

CHERRY-OH

The inspiration for this drink came from the combo of kirsch (a brandy distilled from the fermented juice of morello cherries) and unsweetened black cherry juice – and how those two things seem to really sing when combined with a fruity Prosecco.

Ingredients
60ml (2fl oz) gin
60ml (2fl oz) unsweetened black cherry juice
15ml (½fl oz) kirsch
15ml (½fl oz) Simple Syrup (see page 16)
1 drop of Peychaud's Bitters
30ml (1fl oz) extra dry-style Prosecco
1 morello cherry, to garnish

Instructions
Fill a cocktail shaker with ice. Pour in the gin, cherry juice, kirsch, Simple Syrup and bitters. Shake well and strain into a coupe glass. Top with the Prosecco and garnish with a morello cherry.

CHERRY-OH
Kirsch
wasser
abv 40%

AROMATIC
COCKTAIL
BITTERS

GOLD MEDAL
THE ORIGNAL FORMULA
35% abv 5FL.OZS. 148ml

GIN

GREEN EYES

The tart combination of citrusy-style gin, herbaceous Green Chartreuse and sprightly lemon juice gets a really fun bit of sparkle and sweetness from a fruity, dry-style Prosecco here. And is a great way to usher in spring (or, perhaps, try to hurry it along!).

Ingredients
45ml (1½fl oz) gin
15ml (½fl oz) Green Chartreuse
8ml (¼fl oz) freshly squeezed lemon juice
60ml (2fl oz) dry-style Prosecco
a thin slice of Granny Smith apple, to garnish

Instructions
Fill a cocktail shaker with ice. Pour in the gin, Chartreuse and lemon juice. Shake well and strain into an ice-filled double rocks glass. Top with the Prosecco and garnish with the apple slice.

SHIP TO SHORE

My friend Kevin Rice is an architect. He and his awesome architect wife, Tina Vultaggio, live about three doors down from me and are, quite often, the guinea pigs for liquidy libations I'm attempting to concoct. Kevin also happens to be a pretty good co-creator of cocktails. Sometimes, if I'm just missing something, he can come up with an element that brings the whole thing together. This is one of those cocktails. It sounds like a crazy combo of items, but beneath it all there's this hum of rich ripe and dried fruits that get a boost from both the spicy habanero bitters and extra-dry Prosecco. The name? Rum, Cognac and port historically spent a whole lot of time on boats.

Ingredients
15ml (½fl oz) Jamaican rum
15ml (½fl oz) Cognac
15ml (½fl oz) tawny port
22ml (¾fl oz) freshly squeezed lemon juice
1 bar spoon (1tsp) of orange curaçao
8ml (¼fl oz) Simple Syrup (see page 16)
1 dash of habanero bitters
30ml (1fl oz) extra dry-style Prosecco

Instructions
Fill a cocktail shaker with ice. Pour in the rum, Cognac, port, lemon juice, curaçao, Simple Syrup and habanero bitters. Shake well and strain into a coupe or cocktail glass. Top with the Prosecco.

SHINY NAIL

My Dad, Michael Zavatto, introduced me to the charms of this not very charmingly named cocktail (well, you know, unless you have a thing for rusty nails). But its name isn't because it's a tetanus-dispensing drink; it's for the colour that Drambuie (a honey-and-Scotch liqueur) draws out in it, adding a pretty touch of browny-red to its hue. With this drink, I think it's worth going for a DOCG-status Prosecco from the Valdobbiadene area, where the rocky, marine-deposit soils add a minerally, briny character that fits the drink nicely. I like using a blended Scotch that has a hint of salt and smoke with a fruity base, like Cutty Sark, Famous Grouse or Johnny Walker Red.

Ingredients
75ml (2½fl oz) Scotch
8ml (¼fl oz) Drambuie
60ml (2fl oz) extra dry-style Prosecco
a wide piece of lemon peel, to garnish

Instructions
Fill a double rocks glass with ice. Pour in the Scotch and Drambuie. Give it a little stir. Top with Prosecco and garnish with the lemon peel.

FELICE'S FERRAGOSTO

A few years back, my husband and I went for a visit to my father-in-law's region of Sicily, Agrigento, during the summer celebration there known as Ferragosto (the Roman Catholic celebration that basically kicks off the summer holidays in Italy). After a long day on the beach, the towns come alive at night with music, street fairs and throngs of vacationers strolling around, eating gelato and enjoying the time off from work and school. One of our favourite things to do was grab a seat at an outdoor café within earshot of some live music, spooning out a chilly, espresso-topped affogato, or simply sipping on a little amaretto over ice. This drink brings me right back there.

Ingredients
30ml (1 fl oz) amaretto liqueur
30ml (1 fl oz) freshly squeezed orange juice
2 dashes of orange bitters
90ml (3fl oz) extra dry-style Prosecco
a wide piece of orange peel, to garnish

Instructions
Pour the amaretto, orange juice and bitters into an ice-filled double rocks glass and top with the Prosecco. Give it a little stir and garnish with the orange peel.

COME ON IN

I love the combination of fresh basil and pineapple.
A gently fruit-forward, extra dry- or dry-style Prosecco
boosts all that great sweet herby and tropical flavour
even more. Mionetto makes a non-vintage DOCG version
from Valdobbiadene from the town of Cartizze that has
the perfect combo of notes (floral, herby and a touch
of kiwi-tropical fruit) that goes so nicely with this drink.
(The name? Pineapples are the symbol of welcome!)

Ingredients
45ml (1 ½fl oz) London dry gin
8ml (¼fl oz) Basil Syrup (see page 16)
60ml (2fl oz) unsweetened pineapple juice
2 dashes of lemon bitters
90ml (3fl oz) extra dry- or dry-style Prosecco
a sprig of basil, to garnish
a pineapple wedge, to garnish

Instructions
Pour the gin, Basil Syrup, pineapple juice and lemon bitters
into a cocktail shaker filled with ice. Shake well and strain
into a Collins glass. Top with the Prosecco, garnish with a
sprig of basil and a pineapple wedge and pop in a straw.

POSITANO POP

Italy's picturesque Amalfi Coast has earned its reputation as a vacation dream spot, with its dramatic cliffs jutting from the Sorrentine Peninsula, pretty little beaches – and, of course, ever-flowing bottles of potent, sweet-tart limoncello. This twist on a Champagne cocktail swaps out the Cognac with Positano's popular digestif.

Ingredients
1 sugar cube
4–5 drops of lemon bitters
22ml (¾fl oz) limoncello
90ml (3fl oz) brut-style Prosecco
a lemon twist, to garnish

Instructions
Drop the sugar cube into a Champagne flute. Saturate with the lemon bitters and then break it up using a muddler or the end of a wooden spoon. Pour in the limoncello and top with the Prosecco. Garnish with the lemon twist.

BUBBLY JACK ROSE

Brandy and Prosecco are easy friends. You can riff on the two ingredients adding in other layers of flavour with little fear of failure. The Jack Rose is a great American cocktail that makes good use of something called Applejack – American apple brandy made popular during the colonial era. The gentle presence of residual sugar in an extra dry-level Prosecco works well here to put a bit of fruity sparkle on top of this classic cocktail – and if you really want to fine-tune the flavours, I'm a fan of working with an extra dry-style DOCG version from the Rive di Manzana in Conegliano (Frasinelli's works great), with its rich mouthfeel and orchard-fruit notes. If you can't find Applejack, substitute with Calvados, the famed apple brandy from Normandy.

Ingredients
45ml (1½fl oz) Applejack or Calvados (apple brandy)
8ml (¼fl oz) Grenadine (see page 17)
15ml (½fl oz) freshly squeezed lemon juice
60ml (2fl oz) extra dry-style Prosecco
a lemon twist, to garnish

Instructions
Pour the Applejack, Grenadine and lemon juice into a cocktail shaker filled with ice. Shake well and strain into a coupe or cocktail glass. Top with the Prosecco and garnish with the lemon twist.

GARDEN WALK

Lemon verbena is one of my favourite potted herbs to grow because its aroma is absolutely irresistible and its fast, prolific growth is totally just-add-water rewarding. Its lemony-sweet smell kind of reminds me of Juicy Fruit chewing gum, and it makes the most delicious simple syrup in the world (see page 16 for instructions on how to make simple syrups). Combine it with some gin, a brut-style Prosecco and some celery bitters and you won't know what's more pleasurable – sniffing its pretty aromatics or sipping this lovely refreshing combo. Okay, sipping.

Ingredients
50ml (1¾fl oz) gin
15ml (½fl oz) lemon verbena syrup
15ml (½fl oz) freshly squeezed lemon juice
2 dashes of celery bitters
90ml (3fl oz) brut-style Prosecco
a lemon slice or lemon verbena sprig, to garnish

Instructions
Pour the gin, lemon verbena syrup, lemon juice and celery bitters into a cocktail shaker filled with ice. Shake well and strain into an ice-filled Collins glass. Top with the Prosecco. Garnish with a lemon slice or sprig of lemon verbena (or, heck, both!) and pop in a straw.

SEEDS OF CHANGE

The sweet-tart taste of pomegranate goes gorgeously with a dry, brut-style Prosecco (it's also a great start to a sparkling punch if you need to throw one together in a jiffy!). Think of this as a revved-up Mimosa.

Ingredients
a few pomegranate seeds
30ml (1fl oz) vodka
22ml (¾fl oz) pomegranate liqueur (I use PAMA)
22ml (¾fl oz) freshly squeezed orange juice
90ml (3fl oz) brut-style Prosecco

Instructions
Drop a few pomegranate seeds into a flute. Pour in the vodka, pomegranate liqueur and orange juice and top with the Prosecco.

DANCE PARTY

There are drinks that just go down so easy, they seem to have powers beyond simply tasting delicious. Like, say, one minute you're sipping on this little rum-based Prosecco charmer and the next thing you know you and all your buds are dancing around your living room. This floral, fun, citrusy sparkler promises to do just that.

Ingredients
45ml (1½fl oz) white rum
22ml (¾fl oz) elderflower liqueur
15ml (½fl oz) freshly squeezed lime juice
60ml (2fl oz) brut-style Prosecco
a wide piece of lime peel, to garnish

Instructions
Fill a cocktail shaker with ice. Pour in the rum, elderflower liqueur and lime juice. Shake well and strain into an ice-filled double rocks glass. Top with the Prosecco and garnish with the lime peel.

TIZIANO

Invented in Venice, this sparkling cocktail uses muddled black grapes to create its colour (the inspiration for its name, the 16th-century painter Tiziano Vecellio, was fond of the purplish-red hue that the cocktail's main ingredient adds). Where I live, Concord grapes are prolific and easy to find in the late summer and early autumn, so I use them to make a syrup that adds a fun local twist to this Italian tipple (although any red or black grapes will do).

Ingredients
30ml (1fl oz) Concord Grape Syrup (see page 17)
90–120ml (3–4fl oz) brut-style Prosecco

Instructions
Pour the grape syrup into a flute. Top with the Prosecco.

GRAND AVENUE FROLIC

In the town I grew up in, there is an old hotel called the Chequit, that used to be the site of a great bar where lots and lots of merrymaking occurred on a nightly basis all summer long. It was the 80s. There was lots of neon, asymmetrical hair, Depeche Mode, dancing and drinking of bright, tropical, summery things, like the Madras – a particularly popular tipple among my friends and me. I abandoned it as years went on for less fruity, more 'serious' cocktails. But the thing is, who wants to be so serious when sipping cocktails? Especially bubbly ones. This souped-up Madras is even more delicious with a splash of extra-dry Prosecco. Viva la 80s.

Ingredients
45ml (1½fl oz) vodka
22ml (¾fl oz) cranberry juice
22ml (¾fl oz) freshly squeezed orange juice
30ml (1fl oz) freshly squeezed lime juice
15ml (½fl oz) Cointreau
90ml (3fl oz) extra dry-style Prosecco
a wide piece of lime peel, to garnish

Instructions
Fill a cocktail shaker with ice. Pour in the vodka, cranberry juice, orange and lime juices and Cointreau. Shake well and strain into an ice-filled Collins glass. Top with the Prosecco, garnish with the lime peel and pop in a straw.

BRUT

DOC

PROSECCO

ITALY

750ml   12%abv

MIMOSA SUD

Perhaps one of the easiest cocktails to throw together is that classic brunch staple, the Mimosa. Orange juice, sparkling, boom! You're done. But not only that, you've got something refreshing and festive that never fails to put a smile on everyone's face. Taking a little extra effort, though, in the form of squeezing some fresh juice, makes a world of difference. Here, I like to add a little Italian twist with fresh blood orange juice, for both its flavour and gorgeous colour, along with an extra dry-style Prosecco to add a nice, round fruitiness to the sparkle and pop.

Ingredients
60ml (2fl oz) freshly squeezed blood orange juice
90–120ml (3–4fl oz) brut-style Prosecco

Instructions
Pour the blood orange juice into a flute. Top with the Prosecco.

RISE OF THE MOJITO

Adding a little Prosecco in place of the usual soda water in a Mojito makes this perennial fun favourite even more refreshing (and aromatic!). Definitely veer towards a drier-style Prosecco with a little more minerality (think DOCG Valdobbiadene), as it livens up and plays well with all that fresh, fragrant mint.

Ingredients

7–8 fresh mint leaves, plus an extra sprig to garnish
22ml (¾fl oz) Simple Syrup (see page 16)
22ml (¾fl oz) freshly squeezed lime juice
60ml (2fl oz) white rum
90ml (3fl oz) extra dry-style Prosecco

Instructions

Drop the mint leaves into a cocktail shaker and top with the Simple Syrup. Muddle until the leaves release their natural oils and you start to smell all that nice minty freshness. Add in some ice. Pour in the lime juice and rum and shake well. Strain into an ice-filled Collins glass. Top with the Prosecco, garnish with the mint sprig and pop in a straw.

PUCCINI

You know it's the festive season when bags and small wooden crates of clementines begin to appear at your local greengrocers. They are a smaller, sweeter, seedless offshoot of a mandarin orange, which is the source of citrus for this northern Italian-created sipper. The inventor of this drink was, apparently, one Renato Haussmann, a barman who crafted a new version of the Mimosa during the winter of 1948 in the alpine city of Cortina d'Ampezzo at the Posta Hotel. The name is for Giacomo Puccini; the citrus for the eponymous mandarin heroine of his opera, Turandot. I prefer to switch out the traditional flute for a tulip glass in order to really get a whiff of those lovely clementine aromatics, and use a brut-style Prosecco as clementines are naturally super sweet.

Ingredients
60ml (2fl oz) freshly squeezed clementine juice
90–120ml (3–4fl oz) brut-style Prosecco

Instructions
Pour the fresh clementine juice into a tulip glass. Top with the Prosecco.

OF COURSE

Marinating melon in sweet Marsala wine adds a sweet-savoury kick to the fruit. I like to use honeydew for this recipe, but feel free to use your favourite melon (or whatever kind you happen to have in your house at the time).

Ingredients
170g (6oz) honeydew melon, cut up into cubes
120ml (4fl oz) sweet Marsala wine
90ml (3fl oz) extra dry-style Prosecco

Instructions
Place the melon pieces in a bowl and pour the Marsala wine over them. Cover and refrigerate for 2–4 hours. Purée the mixture in a blender or food processor (you will have more than enough for several drinks; store any extra in a glass, airtight container for a day or two). Pour 60ml (2fl oz) of the mixture into a tulip glass and top with the Prosecco.

SEELBACH
Hotel

LOUISVILLE
KY

THE SEELBACH

Who says whiskey and bubbles can't be friends? This lovely whiskey-centric drink was created by barman Adam Seger in 1995 to provide its namesake hotel (given a spot of fame for its mention by F. Scott Fitzgerald in *The Great Gatsby*) in Louisville, Kentucky, with a much-needed signature cocktail. The result made this drink a classic far and beyond its late 20th-century birth.

Ingredients

30ml (1fl oz) Old Forester bourbon (or your favourite brand)
15ml (½fl oz) triple sec
7 dashes of Angostura bitters
7 dashes of Peychaud's Bitters
90–120ml (3–4fl oz) brut-style Prosecco
an orange twist, to garnish

Instructions

Fill a cocktail shaker with ice. Pour in the bourbon, triple sec and bitters. Stir well and strain into a flute. Top with the Prosecco and garnish with the orange twist.

ROSABEL

Taking a cue from the Kir Royale, a Rosabel uses
Prosecco more as a way of unifying the crème de cassis
and sweet vermouth rather than highlighting the sparkling,
but this pretty red-hued, low-alcohol drink is a great
way to kick off, or even end, an evening. Although the
traditional way of serving it is in a flute, I prefer this drink
over ice with a nice, wide swathe of orange peel.

Ingredients
30ml (1 fl oz) crème de cassis
30ml (1 fl oz) Cocchi Vermouth di Torino
22ml (¾ fl oz) brut-style Prosecco
a wide piece of orange peel, to garnish

Instructions
Combine the crème de cassis and vermouth in an ice-
filled double rocks glass. Give it a little stir and top
with the Prosecco. Garnish with the orange peel.

PINK SGROPPINO

It's summer. It's hot. It's sticky! What you need is internal air-conditioning. You can play around with the sweetness level on this chilly, fruity, kicked-up adult treat depending on where and when you want to have it (before dinner as a palate cleanser, or after as dessert) and change the sorbet flavour for your favourite kind. I like the fun, fruity kick of raspberries here combined with a sweeter-style (aka, dry) Prosecco for an afternoon treat or post-barbecue cap-off.

Ingredients
80g (3oz) raspberry sorbet
22ml (¾fl oz) Gewürztraminer grappa
90ml (3fl oz) dry-style Prosecco
3–4 fresh raspberries, to garnish

Instructions
Put the sorbet, Prosecco and grappa in a cocktail shaker and shake until combined and smooth. Pour into a tulip glass and garnish with the fresh raspberries.

SPARKLING BONAPARTE

Prosecco and Cognac really, really like each other. Maybe it's because they are cousins in grape-based beginnings; maybe it's just that sparkling wine highlights the fruit-centric notes in great brandy. I like the combo here of Cognac and Prosecco with pink grapefruit juice and the underlying orange-y hum of Cointreau.

Ingredients
22ml (¾fl oz) Cognac VS
15ml (½fl oz) Cointreau
30ml (1fl oz) freshly squeezed pink grapefruit juice
30–60ml (1–2fl oz) extra dry-style Prosecco

Instructions
Fill a cocktail shaker with ice. Pour in the Cognac, Cointreau and pink grapefruit juice. Shake well and strain into a coupe glass. Top with the Prosecco.

1849

ORANGE

LIQUEUR

E Cointreau

ANGERS FRANCE

40% alc/vol (80 proof)

IMPORTED

Cognac

FRANCE
COGNAC
VERY SPECIAL
1765

40% vol   70 cl

BREAK THE SILENCE

One of the most pivotal screen stars of the 20th century, Charlie Chaplin somehow managed to make a big impression without uttering a sound. This riff on his namesake cocktail breaks the silence with the festive pop of a Prosecco cork (and, perhaps, the slurp of a straw at the bottom of a glass – it's just that delicious!).

Ingredients
45ml (1½fl oz) sloe gin
15ml (½fl oz) apricot brandy
30ml (1fl oz) freshly squeezed lime juice
15ml (½fl oz) Simple Syrup (see page 16)
30–60ml (1–2fl oz) brut-style Prosecco

Instructions
Fill a cocktail shaker with ice. Pour in the sloe gin, apricot brandy, lime juice and Simple Syrup. Shake well and strain into a coupe or cocktail glass. Top with the Prosecco.

GROWN-UP LEMONADE

This drink is a tiny bit dangerous – it's so refreshing and easy to drink, you'll find it disappears fast. Use a good-quality limoncello (Caravella makes a nice version), or plan ahead (a week to 10 days for maceration) and make your own!

Ingredients
35ml (1¼fl oz) vodka
22ml (¾fl oz) limoncello
3 dashes of lemon bitters
60–90ml (2–3fl oz) brut-style Prosecco
a wide piece of lemon peel, to garnish

Instructions
Fill a double rocks glass with ice. Pour in the vodka, limoncello and bitters. Give it a good stir. Top with the Prosecco and garnish with the lemon peel.

NATURE, NURTURE

Your in-laws are coming over for lunch. You want to show them you're sophisticated, but also interesting. And fun. In other words, you want to give them a glimpse of why their precious offspring has fallen for you. Avoid discussing politics and have one of these at the ready when they walk in the door. It's delicious and refreshing, but the cucumber-tinged Hendrick's, bright addition of lime bitters and pretty sparkle from a brut-style Prosecco make it more interesting than simply gin and juice.

Ingredients
45ml (1½fl oz) Hendrick's gin
22ml (¾fl oz) elderflower liqueur
60ml (2fl oz) unsweetened pineapple juice
2 dashes of lime bitters
60–90ml (2–3fl oz) brut-style Prosecco
a wide piece of lime peel, to garnish

Instructions
Fill a shaker with ice. Pour in the gin, elderflower liqueur, pineapple juice and lime bitters. Give it a good shake and strain into an ice-filled double rocks glass. Top with the Prosecco and garnish with the lime peel.

FIZZY WATERMELON MARGARITA

Watermelon has got to be one of the most thirst-quenching fruits in the entire world. And actually, its name is no accident: the brightly-hued fruit is 92% water. But I don't have to tell you that despite the water, it's not without flavour – and, in this case, flavour that gets wonderfully kicked up with a little extra dry-style Prosecco.

Ingredients
90ml (3fl oz) Watermelon Purée (see page 18)
30ml (1fl oz) silver tequila
15ml (½fl oz) triple sec
22ml (¾fl oz) freshly squeezed lime juice
15ml (½fl oz) Simple Syrup (see page 16)
60ml (2fl oz) extra dry-style Prosecco
3 frozen watermelon cubes, to garnish
a fresh mint sprig, to garnish

Instructions
Combine the Watermelon Purée, tequila, triple sec, lime juice and Simple Syrup in a shaker filled with ice. Shake well and strain into an ice-filled double rocks glass. Top with the Prosecco. Skewer the frozen watermelon cubes onto a single toothpick and garnish with this and the mint sprig.

LEGHORN SPRITZ

Sunny yellow and presented in a gorgeous, tall, slim glass bottle, Galliano got quite a bit of mid-20th century fame for the once-popular Harvey Wallbanger cocktail. But this exotic, sweet, herbaceous liqueur's history goes all the way back to 1896, when it was invented by the brandy producer Arturo Vaccari in the Tuscan city of Livorno, who named his creation for Guiseppe Galliano, a hero of the Italo-Ethiopian War. For reasons I have yet to uncover, Brits like to refer to this city on the Ligurian Sea as Leghorn. But while that might be a mystery, the delicious combo of the lo-fi ingredients below is not.

Ingredients
22ml (¾fl oz) Galliano liqueur
22ml (¾fl oz) Aperol
90ml (3fl oz) brut-style Prosecco
a wide piece of lemon peel, to garnish

Instructions
Pour the Galliano and Aperol into an ice-filled double rocks glass. Give it a little stir and top with the Prosecco. Garnish with the lemon peel.

SUNSHINE SUPERMAN

One evening, my husband Dan came home after a particularly stressful, horrible work day and the look on his face said to me, oh dear, that man needs something to put a smile on his face. And rum? Well, if rum can't put you in a better mood, I don't know what can. I had a little leftover ice wine from a dinner party, and was struck by inspiration: the caramelized, vanilla, dried fruit flavours in the rum combined with the apricot notes of the ice wine and the bright, buoyant fruit in a dry-style Prosecco sounded like just the trick. It was! Spouse happy, new favourite cocktail created. Win-win.

Ingredients
45ml (1½fl oz) Jamaican rum
15ml (½fl oz) ice wine
30ml (1fl oz) brut-style Prosecco
a wide piece of orange peel, to garnish

Instructions
Pour the rum and ice wine into an ice-filled double rocks glass. Give it a little stir and top with the Prosecco. Garnish with the orange peel.

Common in places like Germany and the Finger Lakes region of New York State, ice wine is exactly what it sounds like – it's made from grapes left on their vines long after the normal harvest time so that they literally freeze. When this happens, the sugars inside them become more concentrated and almost honey-like, so when they are quickly crushed after picking, the result is a near-syrupy, decadent dessert wine that will make you swoon.

BORDER PASS

I like a Paloma as much, or possibly even more, than a Margarita. It's so simple and makes ample use of grapefruit juice (a plus in my book!). This souped-up version adds a little lime and simple syrup, along with a bubbly burst of dry-style Prosecco.

Ingredients
30ml (1fl oz) freshly squeezed grapefruit juice
8ml (¼fl oz) freshly squeezed lime juice
45ml (1½fl oz) reposado tequila
15ml (½fl oz) Simple Syrup (see page 16)
90ml (3fl oz) dry-style Prosecco

Instructions
Fill a shaker with ice. Pour in the grapefruit juice, lime juice, tequila and Simple Syrup. Shake well and strain into an ice-filled Collins glass. Top with the Prosecco and add a straw.

ISLAY SOUR

One recent spring evening on an unseasonably hot day where I live in New York, I had some pink grapefruit sitting around in the refrigerator. I was trying to figure out what to make to go with some fish I had for dinner and considered putting the grapefruit on the grill – it caramelizes the sugars and makes a nice smoky-sweet accent. But then I got to thinking: wouldn't it be cool to make a refreshing drink that emulated that smoky grapefruit flavour using mezcal or Islay Scotch? The answer was yes, yes it was! The drink on its own is lovely, but add a splash of brut-style Prosecco, and the flavours are really lifted up. I prefer the single malt Uigeadail from the wonderful Ardbeg distillery in Islay here, because its strong smoke component is beautifully balanced by a rich, fruity characteristic in the malt.

Ingredients
30ml (1fl oz) Ardbeg 'Uigeadail' single malt Scotch
30ml (1fl oz) pink grapefruit juice
8ml (¼fl oz) Simple Syrup (see page 16)
30–60ml (1–2fl oz) brut-style Prosecco
a wide piece of pink grapefruit peel, to garnish

Instructions
Fill a cocktail shaker with ice cubes. Pour in the Scotch, grapefruit juice and Simple Syrup. Shake for 20 seconds. Strain slowly into an ice-filled double rocks glass. Top with the Prosecco and garnish with the grapefruit peel.

BUNNAHABHAIN

CAOL ILA

BRUICHLADDICH

BOWMORE

ARDMORE

ARDBEG
LAGAVULIN

LAPHROAIG

ISLAY
SOUR

SUNDAY IN THE PARK

The delicate, soft floral notes of chamomile combined
with a brut-style Prosecco make such a lovely combo,
all they really need are some subtle accents via a little
Cointreau and a touch of ginger. Combine the first three
ingredients in a chilled thermos, grab a bottle of Prosecco
and bring this concoction to your next picnic in the park.

Ingredients
90ml (3fl oz) unsweetened chamomile tea
15ml (½fl oz) Cointreau
8ml (¼fl oz) Ginger Simple Syrup (see page 17)
90ml (3fl oz) extra dry-style Prosecco
a slice of fresh peach or orange, to garnish

Instructions
Fill a Collins glass with ice. Pour in the tea, Cointreau
and Ginger Simple Syrup. Stir for a few seconds and
top with the Prosecco. Pop in a straw and garnish
with a thin slice of fresh peach or orange.

TODAY'S WINNER

This twist on a classic Brandy Crusta gets its little tropical update from some unsweetened pineapple juice and tiki bitters, which, depending on the producer, tend to have an exotic edge to them, with spices and notes of cinnamon, allspice, ginger and citrus. Combined with an extra dry-style Prosecco, this winner of a sipper will take your taste buds swiftly over the finish line.

Ingredients
45ml (1½fl oz) Cognac
8ml (¼fl oz) Luxardo Maraschino liqueur
8ml (¼fl oz) triple sec
8ml (¼fl oz) freshly squeezed lemon juice
15ml (½fl oz) unsweetened pineapple juice
3 dashes of tiki bitters
60ml (2fl oz) extra dry-style Prosecco
a strawberry, to garnish

Instructions
Combine the Cognac, Maraschino liqueur, triple sec, lemon juice, pineapple juice and tiki bitters in an ice-filled shaker. Shake well and strain into a tulip glass. Top with the Prosecco and garnish with a strawberry.

LUXE LIFE

If your only familiarity with the word 'maraschino' is of the unnaturally red, super-sweet cherries that top a sundae, you're in for a big treat. Maraschino liqueur is distilled from marasca cherries, stones and all. The final result is a beautiful, brandy-like beauty that smells like pretty flowers and nuts – and is Prosecco's absolute best buddy in the glass. No lie. Maybe even more than Cognac. So much so, you really don't need anything else with it, the two together are such a great combo. Pop in another one of Italy's famed cherries as a garnish, and you've got an easy, impressive cocktail to quickly serve a crowd. With a two-ingredient cocktail such as this one, it may be worth your while to upgrade to a DOCG Prosecco. Seek out one from the eastern part of the DOCG, where the soils encourage more of a stone fruit and mineral profile in the wine.

Ingredients
1 Amarena cherry
30ml (1fl oz) Luxardo Maraschino liqueur
90–120ml (3–4fl oz) extra dry-style Prosecco

Instructions
Drop the cherry into a flute. Pour in the Luxardo Maraschino liqueur and top with the Prosecco.

AIR MAIL

If you've never had the pleasure of flipping through Esquire's *Handbook for Hosts* (first published in 1949; revisited in 1977), you're in for a time-warp treat. Not only is it chock-full of hostess-with-the-mostest recipes, advice on equipment and a funny picture of a naked lady, it also offers up coin tricks to entertain your guests and drink recipes like this little gem.

Ingredients
60ml (2fl oz) golden rum
22ml (¾fl oz) freshly squeezed lime juice
15ml (½fl oz) Honey Syrup (see page 17)
90–120ml (3–4fl oz) brut-style Prosecco
a lime twist, to garnish

Instructions
Combine the rum, lime juice and Honey Syrup in an ice-filled shaker. Shake well and strain into an ice-filled Collins glass. Top with the Prosecco and garnish with a lime twist.

DON JUANCHO NIETO MELENDEZ
TEREPAIMA
VENEZUELA

AIR MAIL

RESERVA

70cl   40%

RUM

honey

COUNTESS CRAWLEY

Oh, Countess Crawley. You of the high-stacked hair
and demure Victorian dresses. But while the Countess
is ever the straight-backed, pursed-lipped arbiter of
manners and good taste, beneath that buttoned up,
feather-accented, begloved exterior is the woman who
had an affair with a Russian prince. That Countess?
She'd like a genteel little cocktail with her name on it.
A little dose of lavender-hued crème de violette, fresh
lemon and sprightly Prosecco seems just the trick.

Ingredients

22ml (¾fl oz) crème de violette
22ml (¾fl oz) freshly squeezed lemon juice
30ml (1fl oz) gin (for this recipe, I prefer something floral,
  such as NY Distilling's Dorothy Parker American Gin)
60ml (2fl oz) extra dry-style Prosecco
a blackberry, to garnish

Instructions

Combine the crème de violette, lemon juice and gin in an
ice-filled shaker. Shake well and strain into a tulip glass.
Top with the Prosecco and garnish with a blackberry.

HOW BLUE AM I

I wrote my book, *Forager's Cocktails*, because I suspected that there were a lot of people like me out there: that is, folks who might be brave enough to pick up stinging nettles to see what they might inspire, but also those who really relish what to me is the kernel of the whole idea – using fresh, in-season items, be they from a woodland hike or a safari through your local farmer's market. You can forage for wild blueberries not too far from where I live, but you can also nab some pretty nice ones at the greengrocer. And picking off a handful of fresh basil leaves? Ahhh – such a beautiful scent and totally great combo with the fruit, lemon juice and Prosecco!

Ingredients
2oz (60g) fresh blueberries, plus 3–4 to garnish, rinsed
15ml (½fl oz) Basil Simple Syrup (see page 16)
45ml (1½fl oz) vodka
22ml (¾fl oz) freshly squeezed lemon juice
90ml (3fl oz) brut-style Prosecco

Instructions
Drop the blueberries into a shaker. Add the Simple Syrup and muddle thoroughly. Fill with ice, add the vodka and lemon juice and shake well. Strain through a fine mesh sieve into an ice-filled double rocks glass. Top with the Prosecco and garnish with the remaining blueberries.

TEQUILA SUNRISE & SHINE

Like the Old Fashioned and other cocktails that were invented at the turn of, or early part of the 20th century, the Tequila Sunrise's original demure combo of tequila, crème de cassis, lime juice and soda water got entirely lost in the shuffle of the sweet and lowdown 70s. Swap the soda water for a brut-style Prosecco and this classic cocktail sparkles even brighter from the first sip.

Ingredients

45ml (1 ½fl oz) silver tequila
22ml (¾fl oz) crème de cassis
15ml (½fl oz) freshly squeezed lime juice
60–90ml (2–3fl oz) brut-style Prosecco
a lime twist, to garnish

Instructions

Combine the tequila, crème de cassis and lime juice in an ice-filled shaker. Shake well and strain into an ice-filled double rocks glass. Top with the Prosecco and garnish with the lime twist.

70s TEQUILA SUNRISE

Now, before you go kicking the popularized sweet 'n sticky version of the Tequila Sunrise to the curb, consider instead just giving it a little fresh intervention. High-fructose corn syrup juices and mixers? Ick. Grab a couple of oranges, mix up some easy-peasy homemade grenadine and take the shame out of that Sunrise. With a little brut-style Prosecco (going dry in sparkling style here adds some nice balance to the drink's inherent fruitiness), this updated 70s sipper becomes a whole new modern-day hit.

Ingredients
45ml (1½fl oz) reposado tequila
60ml (2fl oz) freshly squeezed orange juice
8ml (¼fl oz) Grenadine (see page 17)
60–90ml (2–3fl oz) brut-style Prosecco
an orange slice, to garnish

Instructions
Pour the tequila, orange juice and Grenadine into an ice-filled highball glass. Give it a good stir and top with the Prosecco. Garnish with an orange slice and pop in a straw.

FELIX'S OTHER FIZZ

The classic Kir cocktail was invented by, and subsequently named after, the Canon Felix Kir, mayor of Burgundy and champion of all the delicious things that come from that lovely area of France, like crème de cassis and the traditional Kir (that uses a still white wine made from the grape Aligote). Swap out the latter for a little sparkly Cremant de Bourgogne, and you've got yourself a Kir Royale. And as long as we're riffing, Prosecco makes a pretty lovely substitute – just make sure you go with a brut style, as the cocktail is not meant to be sweet. And if you can find yourself a bottle of extra brut-style? Go for it! Your refreshed senses will thank you.

Ingredients
8ml (¼fl oz) crème de cassis
120ml (4fl oz) brut- or extra brut-style Prosecco
a raspberry, to garnish

Instructions
Pour the crème de cassis into a flute. Top with the Prosecco and garnish with a raspberry.

KIWI COOLER

The soft, fleshy texture of kiwi fruit responds well to a little time in the freezer. Whiz it up with a gin like Hendrick's (with its pretty cucumber and floral notes) and a little mint simple syrup, top with a glug of extra dry-style Prosecco, and you have a super-chilly, sparkly cooler ripe for the quenching.

Ingredients
4 kiwi slices, just frozen (about 1 kiwi),
   plus 1 unfrozen slice to garnish
15ml (½fl oz) Mint Simple Syrup (see page 16)
8ml (¼fl oz) freshly squeezed lime juice
30ml (1fl oz) Hendrick's gin
60–90ml (2–3fl oz) extra dry-style Prosecco
a fresh mint sprig, to garnish

Instructions
Remove the kiwi slices from the freezer when they are just starting to harden. Drop in a blender or food processer with the Mint Syrup and lime juice, and blend until smooth. Strain through a fine-mesh sieve and pour into a tulip glass. Top with the Prosecco and garnish with a slice of kiwi and a mint sprig.

KEY PUNCH

(serves 12–14)

Every winter, I head down to Key West, Florida, at the southernmost tip of the United States. When you fly in over the blue gulf, looking at the sailboats dotting the water and all the little islands (or keys) that lead up to Key West, any stress that you might have carried with you onto the plane drops right off once the wheels hit the ground among the swaying palms and hilarious famed crowing roosters. It's the kind of place, with its abundance of the petite Key Lime fruit, that makes you thoroughly understand why Ernest Hemingway found his way down there and lingered. The following is my riff on a large-format Hemingway Daiquiri – with bubbles, because Key West is nothing if not a super fun town.

Ingredients
1 ice ring (see page 19)
240ml (8fl oz) white rum
120ml (4fl oz) triple sec
120ml (4fl oz) freshly squeezed lime juice
480ml (16fl oz) unsweetened pineapple juice
120ml (4fl oz) Simple Syrup (see page 16)
1 x 750ml (26fl oz) bottle of extra dry-style Prosecco
1 lime, sliced into thin rings

Instructions
Place the ice ring into a punch bowl. Combine the first 5 ingredients. Give them a gentle stir. Pour in the Prosecco. Garnish with lime slices. Ladle into punch cups and serve.

CHRISTMAS BRUNCH PUNCH

(serves 12–14)

Red, bubbly and entirely festive, this spicy punch is the perfect crowd-pleaser, whether you're inviting family and friends into your own home (which, really, is the genius of punch – it keeps you from having to constantly worry about ingredients for a million different mixed drinks), or looking for something to take to a party you're attending to help your host enjoy the party, too!

Ingredients
1 ice ring (see page 19)
120ml (4fl oz) pomegranate liqueur (I use PAMA)
480ml (16fl oz) pomegranate juice
120ml (4fl oz) pear juice
120ml (4fl oz) freshly squeezed lemon juice
60ml (2fl oz) Cinnamon Simple Syrup (see page 17)
1 x 750ml (26fl oz) bottle of brut-style Prosecco
fresh pomegranate seeds, to garnish

Instructions
Place the ice ring into a punch bowl. Combine the first 5 ingredients. Give them a gentle stir. Pour in the Prosecco. Garnish with the pomegranate seeds. Ladle into punch cups and serve.

A great way to make this punch even more festive is to wet the rim of 12–14 rocks glasses with lemon juice (use the lemons you squeezed for the juice). Combine 100 grams (3 ounces) sugar with 1 tablespoon ground cinnamon on a flat plate, and dip the rims of the glasses in the sugar mixture. Allow to dry and set out for your guests to fill with punch.

FIZZY LEMONADE PUNCH

(serves 12–14)

Great for an afternoon party or Sunday brunch with friends. Whip up this easy, lemony punch to impress a crowd without having to put in very much effort!

Ingredients
1 ice ring (see page 19)
480ml (16fl oz) gin
240ml (8fl oz) freshly squeezed lemon juice
8ml (¼fl oz) orange flower water
120ml (4fl oz) Mint Simple Syrup (see page 16)
1 x 750ml (26fl oz) bottle of brut-style Prosecco
1 lemon, sliced into thin rings

Instructions
Place the ice ring into a punch bowl. Combine the first 4 ingredients. Give them a gentle stir. Pour in the Prosecco. Garnish with lemon slices. Ladle into punch cups and serve.

SPARKLING SIDECAR PUNCH

(Serves 10)

This is another classic cocktail that translates well into a larger format drink for a crowd – and is even more delicious with the addition of a brut-style Prosecco. While you can make most of the punch ahead of time, remember not to add the Prosecco until just before your guests arrive. That way, the bubbles will stay bubbly for a while after they arrive.

Ingredients
1 ice ring (see page 19)
240ml (8fl oz) brandy
60ml (2fl oz) triple sec
180ml (6fl oz) freshly squeezed lemon juice
120ml (4fl oz) Simple Syrup (see page 16)
1 x 750ml (26fl oz) bottle of brut-style Prosecco
1 lemon, sliced into thin rings

Instructions
Place the ice ring into a punch bowl. Combine the first 4 ingredients. Give them a gentle stir. Pour in the Prosecco. Garnish with the lemon slices. Ladle into punch cups and serve.

GREYHOUND PUNCH

(serves 12-14)

Modern versions of the Greyhound more often than not use vodka – a blank slate for the puckery citrus of the grapefruit juice. However, if you're a gin lover (like me!), feel free to sub in a citrusy-style gin.

Ingredients
1 ice ring (see page 19)
240ml (8fl oz) vodka
480ml (16fl oz) grapefruit juice
120ml (4fl oz) Honey-Basil Syrup (see page 17)
1 x 750ml (26fl oz) bottle of extra dry-style Prosecco
1 grapefruit, sliced into rings and then cut into half-moons

Instructions
Place the ice ring into a punch bowl. Combine the first 3 ingredients. Give them a gentle stir. Pour in the Prosecco. Garnish with grapefruit slices. Ladle into punch cups and serve.

BARDSTOWN PUNCH

(serves 20–24)

Be it in Scotland, Ireland, the United States, Canada or Japan, tea (iced or hot) spiked with whiskey is enjoyed, and it is a cross-cultural urge for good reason. It's delicious. This recipe is a nod to Kentucky, a place that some of the great American whiskies have long called home, and where the tradition of sweet tea is a summertime given.

Ingredients
1 ice ring (see page 19)
360ml (12fl oz) bourbon
1.1 litres (40fl oz) unsweetened peach tea
120ml (4fl oz) freshly squeezed lemon juice
180ml (6fl oz) Honey Syrup (see page 17)
1 x 750ml (26fl oz) bottle of extra dry-style Prosecco
1–2 peaches, cut into thin slices

Instructions
Place the ice ring into a punch bowl. Combine the first 4 ingredients. Give them a gentle stir. Pour in the Prosecco. Garnish with the peach slices. Ladle into punch cups and serve.

INDEX

CREDITS

Amy Zavatto would like to thank:
Editor Hazel Eriksson, for her amazingly good humour,
kindness and patience. You made what potentially
could have been a really tough process at a really
tough time in my life a joy from start to finish – thank
you, lady. I owe you some seriously good Prosecco.

Alan Tardi, the US Ambassador to Conegliano Valdobbiadene,
for sharing his knowledge, allowing me to feel like I was smack
in the middle of a hilly vineyard and making me love Prosecco
even more than I did. And Stefanie Schwalb and the Gregory
White team in New York City for their invaluable help, resources
and generosity. To you all, I raise my glass!

Linda Zavatto and Laura Zavatto – the kind of kick-ass
sisters you could only dream up, but they're really mine.
Pearls, both of you.

Dan Marotta – for being my best critic, loyal taster of
experiments (some better than others), best friend and the
sparkle in all of my days. Love you, always.

Ruby Taylor would like to thank:
Total babes Lucy and Eddie, and the
dream team in LG1.